# Dr. Richard Osibanjo

# 5 Essential Things Every Leader Must Get Right

*To my wonderful wife,
Dr. Oyinda Osibanjo,
and our two amazing sons,
David and Daniel.*

# Table of Contents

Introduction. . . . . . . . . . . . . . . . . . . . . . . . . . . . 7

#1 Have a Compelling Vision. . . . . . . . . . . . . . . . 12

#2 Develop Your Leadership Identity. . . . . . . . . . 16

#3 Become Rejection Proof . . . . . . . . . . . . . . . . 20

#4 Be Courageous. . . . . . . . . . . . . . . . . . . . . . . 24

#5 Cultivate Membership . . . . . . . . . . . . . . . . . 30

Closing . . . . . . . . . . . . . . . . . . . . . . . . . . . . . . 36

My Action Plan. . . . . . . . . . . . . . . . . . . . . . . . 37

# 5 Essential Things Every Leader Must Get Right

The world is changing; are you changing with it?

We are experiencing a global pandemic disruption that has changed our perspectives and beliefs about relationships, how we live, and where we work. In particular:

- The balance of power has shifted from employers to employees.

- The employee value proposition has shifted from "work for me" to "work with me."

- Employees favor a hybrid model versus going back to the office full time.

- Employees are rethinking their purpose—they are searching for meaning, not activity. In particular, millennials are interested in working with purpose-driven companies (contribute to resolving environmental, social, and governance issues) rather than those focused only on shareholder value.

In their book, "Lead and Disrupt," O'Reilly and Tushman studied "Why do successful firms find it difficult to adapt in the face of change—to innovate?" The authors found that the problems weren't strategy,

# 5 Essential Things Every Leader Must Get Right

resources, technology, or luck. "It has everything to do with leadership—and how leaders act in the face of change." As we move forward into the post-pandemic world, organizations will thrive or become obsolete based on how leadership quickly adapts to this new normal.

Think about any successful business story, and you will hear stories of great leaders who inspired their teams to do great things. In the same vein, think about any business failure story—you will hear stories of failed leadership. Businesses thrive or fail due to leadership. It starts with you if you want to bring about lasting change—shift mindsets, influence behaviors, and accelerate results. Leading yourself exceptionally well—have a compelling vision, develop your leadership identity, become rejection-proof, be courageous, and cultivate membership. Leadership's attitude to change will determine whether they successfully translate their vision into reality in the post-pandemic world.

The Five Essential Things Every Leader Must Get Right are simple, digestible, and practical tips from over 20 years of leadership and organizational development experience partnering with Fortune 500 executives and leaders from all works of life. These insights will help you accelerate your impact by focusing on the critical drivers of organizational change. Bottom line: being an example is a powerful way to pull others up with you—it creates an environment people can bring their best selves, develop deep relationships, and do meaningful work.

Pause and reflect on the five essential leadership exercises and create your action plan as you read this book. I hope this book provides you with insights that help you make maximum impact and live your best life. In Gandhi's words, "Be the change you want to see in the world." You are the leader you have been waiting for. Let's get after it.

> I am more than a statistic.
> I can make a difference.
> I will be the change.

*- Dr. Richard Osibanjo*

# 5 Essential Things Every Leader Must Get Right

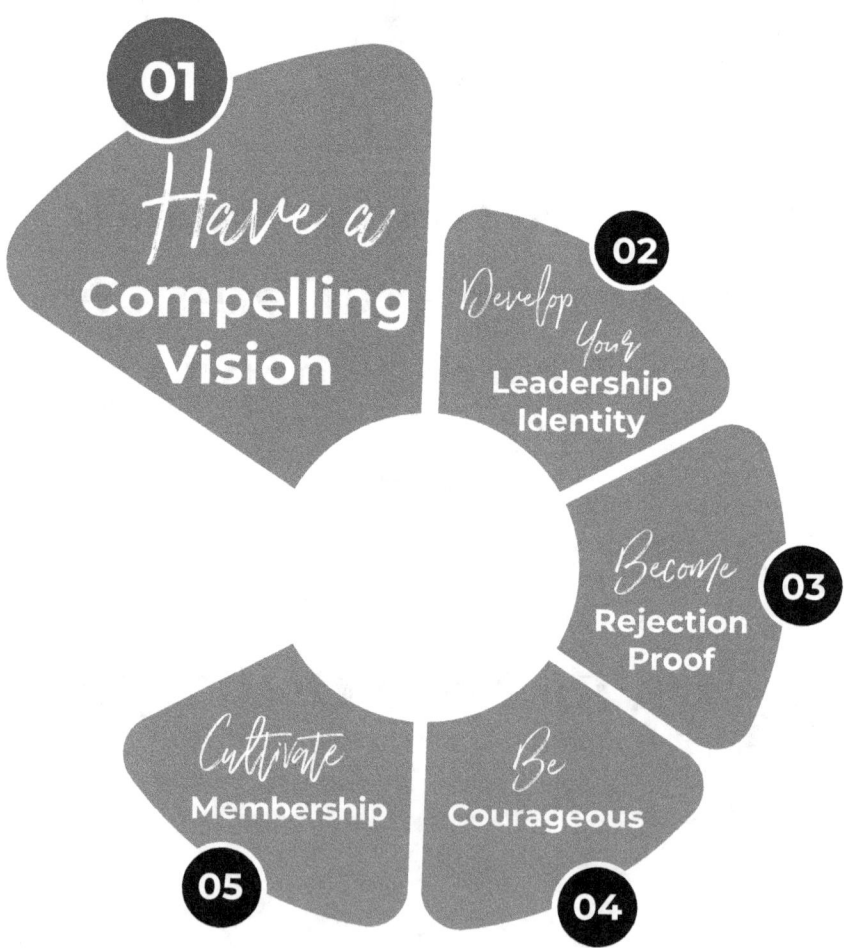

01 Have a **Compelling Vision**

02 Develop Your **Leadership Identity**

03 Become **Rejection Proof**

04 Be **Courageous**

05 Cultivate **Membership**

## #1 Have a compelling vision

What is your vision? Have you discovered something you can pour your life into? Dr. Oleg Konovalov, a leadership expert and author of "The Vision Code," said only about 0.1% of business, social or political leaders have a vision. Think about that.

When there is no vision, organizations become bloated—they become everything to everybody. They seek compromise instead of prioritizing, become lethargic in executing, remain stuck in old thinking, and become grounded by indecision. Having a compelling vision is what distinguishes leaders and organizations from the competition. Anyone can flip on a light switch, but it was Thomas Edison's vision of commercializing the light bulb that changed the world. Does your organization's vision excite you? If not, don't expect your team to be excited about it either.

According to Naina Dhingra, a partner in McKinsey, "70% of employees now demand purposeful work. "These purpose-driven employees are 6.5x more likely to report higher resilience, 6x to stay at the company, 1.5x likely to go above and beyond." Finding meaning, not activity, is non-negotiable for your team and employees. Also, organizational leaders must look beyond compensation to engage their employees. Instead, they must help employees align their purpose to the corporate purpose.

Alan Mulally led Ford's transformation from near bankruptcy into one of the world's leading automakers. To turn around Ford, he went back to Henry Ford's original vision for starting the company—building quality cars that are affordable and available to everyone. Mulally understood that to aim at everything was to aim at nothing. The clarity of his vision (One Ford strategy) activated employees because they knew where the company was going, why it was going there, and what they needed to do to get there. The result? Ford's stock price increased by over 1800%, moving from a low of $1.01 in 2006 to $18.37 in 2014. Leaders will come and go, but their vision will outlive them.

## Food For Thought

Vision is the bridge that connects the past to the future. When there is a vision, organizations flourish. When there is no vision, organizations perish.

- Does your organization have a simple, clear, and inspirational purpose?

- Is your organizational purpose and vision aligned to your purpose and vision?

- Does your organization's vision excite you?

- Is your leadership vision a shared vision, or is it top-down?

- Who else needs to be involved in this?

# 5 Essential Things Every Leader Must Get Right

01 Have a Compelling Vision

02 Develop Your Leadership Identity

03 Become Rejection Proof

04 Be Courageous

05 Cultivate Membership

## #2 Develop your Leadership Identity

Many people were skeptical about Alan Mulally leading the Ford motor company. As the former CEO of Boeing, an aircraft business, he was considered an outsider to the auto industry. During his first news conference at the Ford world headquarters in Dearborn, Michigan, a local reporter asked him how he could successfully tackle the complex automobile business he was unfamiliar with. Mulally responded, "An automobile has about 10,000 moving parts, right? An airplane has two million, and it has to stay up in the air." His clever response silenced his critics.

One thing that Mulally had going for him was his leadership identity. He knew what he was good at, understood the environment he needed to thrive, and believed in his abilities. If you don't know your leadership identity, you become a victim of other people's opinions of what they think it should be. How often have you said no to an opportunity because you let the voices of doubt, inadequacy, "I am not ready," hypotheticals, and fear take over? It doesn't matter how you got to the leadership table. Now that you are at the table act like you belong and deserve to be there. Embrace your uniqueness and be unapologetic about unleashing your creativity. What is your leadership identity? What activities or causes energize you? What is your message to the world? Who needs to hear it? What do people come to you for help for?

## Food For Thought

It is not uncommon to follow the blueprint of your leadership heroes during the early stages of your leadership journey. Ultimately, the goal is to discover your leadership style—what works for you and has the biggest impact. To begin, reflect on the following questions:

- What are your superpowers?

- What drains your energy?

- Who are the leaders that you admire?

- What qualities do you admire about them?

- Why do you admire these qualities?

- What lessons can you embrace from these leaders?

# 5 Essential Things Every Leader Must Get Right

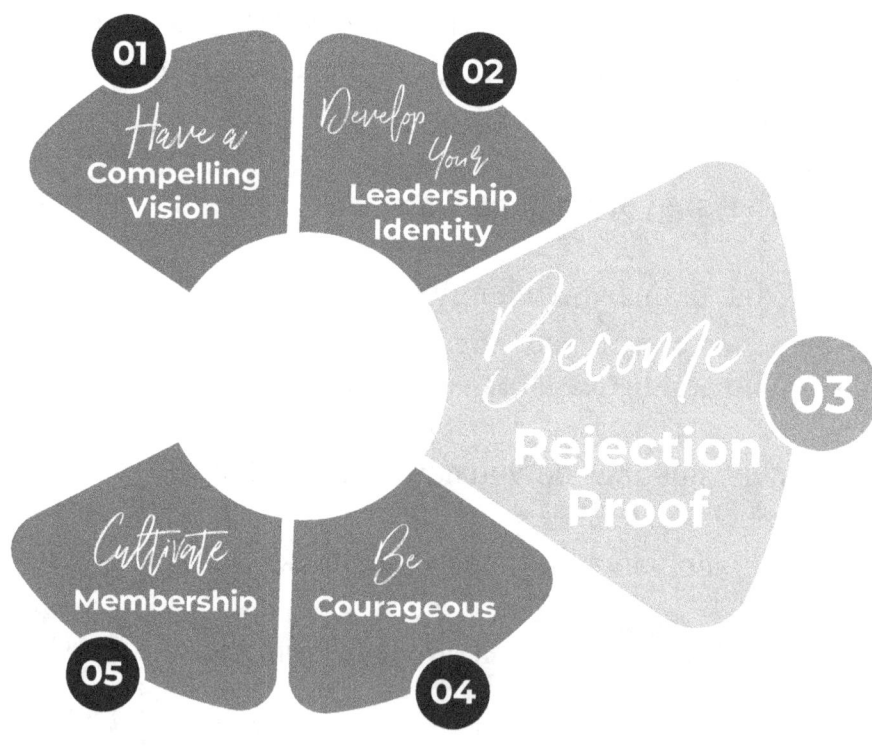

01 Have a Compelling Vision
02 Develop Your Leadership Identity
03 Become Rejection Proof
04 Be Courageous
05 Cultivate Membership

## #3 Become Rejection Proof

No one wants to be rejected. The fear of rejection has crippled many leaders and sent many dreams to the grave. Dr. Myles Munroe shared this insight of what happens when the fear of rejection and failing has the upper hand in our lives. "The graveyard is the richest place on earth because it is here that you will find all the hopes and dreams that were never fulfilled, the books that were never written, the songs that were never sung, the inventions that were never shared, the cures that were never discovered, all because someone was too afraid to take that first step, keep with the problem, or determined to carry out their dream." If you do not want to add to the grave statistics, dare to become rejection proof.

Walt Disney was fired from the Kansas City Star in 1919 because his editor said, "He lacked imagination and had no good ideas." Oprah Winfrey was a news reporter. Her boss fired her because she couldn't sever her emotions from her stories. Twelve publishers rejected J.K. Rowling's "Harry Potter and the Philosopher's Stone" manuscript before one publisher took a chance on her.

As you can see from above, rejection is someone else's perspective or opinion. Oprah, Disney, and Rowling didn't allow other people's opinions to become their facts. They believed the only limits that existed were the ones they placed on themselves. It is human to build walls around yourself when you feel rejected, but walls also shut you out from the world. Imagine what the world would be missing if Walt Disney gave up on his ideas, if Oprah kept emotion out of her stories, or Harry Potter never got published. So what are you holding back for fear of being rejected?

## Food For Thought

- What stories or beliefs are you holding onto that are not serving your interests?

- What experiences, stories, or beliefs do you need to accomplish your goals?

- What small risks can you take to condition yourself to take bigger risks?

# 5 Essential Things Every Leader Must Get Right

01 Have a Compelling Vision

02 Develop Your Leadership Identity

03 Become Rejection Proof

04 Be Courageous

05 Cultivate Membership

## #4 Be Courageous

As of the time of this writing, Russia is invading the democratic country of Ukraine. The Zelenskyy effect—the fearless response of Volodymyr Zelenskyy, the Ukrainian president, and the Ukrainian people has drawn worldwide admiration. The world is seeing firsthand the unbroken spirit of the Ukrainian people despite the intense bombing, increasing causalities, and nearly three million refugees have fled to neighboring countries. Several countries have offered the president asylum, but he has chosen to stand his ground and fight for the future of his country.

Zelenskyy is not military trained. He was a former actor and comedian before he became the president of Ukraine on May 20, 2019. Today, Zelensky has become one of the most consequential presidents of our lifetime. According to Mark Twain, "It's not the size of the dog in the fight, it's the size of the fight in the dog." Zelenskyy's courage has inspired and strengthened the resolve of Ukrianians, global leaders, and people worldwide. According to CNBC, "The Group of Seven, or G-7, major economies have imposed unprecedented punitive sanctions against the Central Bank of Russia along with widespread measures by the West against the country's oligarchs and officials." In a show of support

# 24    5 Essential Things Every Leader Must Get Right

for Ukraine and democracies worldwide, businesses and institutions are cutting ties with Russia. Also, the United Nations General Assembly voted overwhelmingly to reprimand Russia for invading Ukraine and demanded an end to the fighting and the withdrawal of Russia's military forces.

Throughout history, we have seen how one courageous person can move mountains. For example, Mandela's audacity to defy the apartheid government led to the freedom of South Africa. Gandhi's nonviolent resistance led to India's Independence from the British. Martin Luther King Jr.'s dream speech was a tipping point in America's Civil Rights Movement. Malala's fight for girls' education and Greta Thunberg's climate change challenge to world leaders make a difference in today's world. You can see from these leaders that courage is the down payment to enter your desired future. How are you showing up as a leader? Are you inspiring commitment among your leadership team and employees? Below are highlights of the Zelenskyy leadership effect that you can incorporate in your organization:

- **Connection is king in show business**: To be a successful comedian, you must connect with the heads and hearts of your audience. Zelensky used his ability to communicate with his audience to win over the Ukrainian people to become the president. Also, amidst the invasion, Zelensky is still inspiring his people, winning the court of public opinion, and challenging global leaders to do more.

- **There is no traditional path to leadership**: Zelenskyy was a former actor and comedian. That didn't stop him from pursuing his dream of becoming the president of Ukraine. So, do not allow your nontraditional credentials to stop you from pursuing your goals. All you need is the belief and courage to pursue your dreams to turn them into reality.

- **Visibility matters**: As the invasion intensified, Zelensky has been visible to the Ukrainian people and the world, thus putting his life at risk. He has shown that he is a leader who leads from the trenches and not behind walls. His actions demonstrate that he cares for his people and country more than his comfort. Being a visible leader in crisis has won him the loyalty and admiration of his people and the world.

- **Courage is contagious**: Zelenskyy wasn't asking his citizens to do what he wasn't willing to do himself. He is leading by the power of his example. He rejected asylum offers from Europe. In Zelensky's words, "I will stay in my country, and if I die, I will die with my soldiers." His actions have inspired the Ukrainian people to stand their ground and fight for their Nation's freedom. Courage is contagious, and it changes the trajectory of nations when leaders act boldly.

The Zelenskyy effect can be boiled down to Gandhi's words, "Be the change you want to see in the world." Becoming a courageous leader means standing up for what is right versus popular. It is pursuing and giving your dreams a fighting chance. In the end, you have to decide which is worse—stepping out of your comfort zone or experiencing the pain of regret for not trying to be all you can become. The actions you take today will determine the possibilities you create tomorrow.

## Food For Thought

There was a scene in the HBO hit show, Game of Thrones. The child asked his father, "Can a man still be brave even if he's afraid?" His father replied, "That is the only time a man can be brave." Courage is like a muscle; you need to develop it to strengthen it. It takes courage to transform your ideas into action. It takes courage to say "no" to the things that don't matter so you can "yes" to the things that count. Courage is required to have crucial conversations that improve performance and productivity. Courage is the key ingredient to pursue and live your best life.

- What's possible if you could be more courageous?
- Are you role modeling the change you want people to make?
- How is fear holding you back from pursuing your best life?
- Do your people see and feel that you care about them?
- What are two to three actions you can take to cultivate courage as a leader?
- What is one thing you could do daily over the next 90 days to grow your courage muscle?

# 5 Essential Things Every Leader Must Get Right

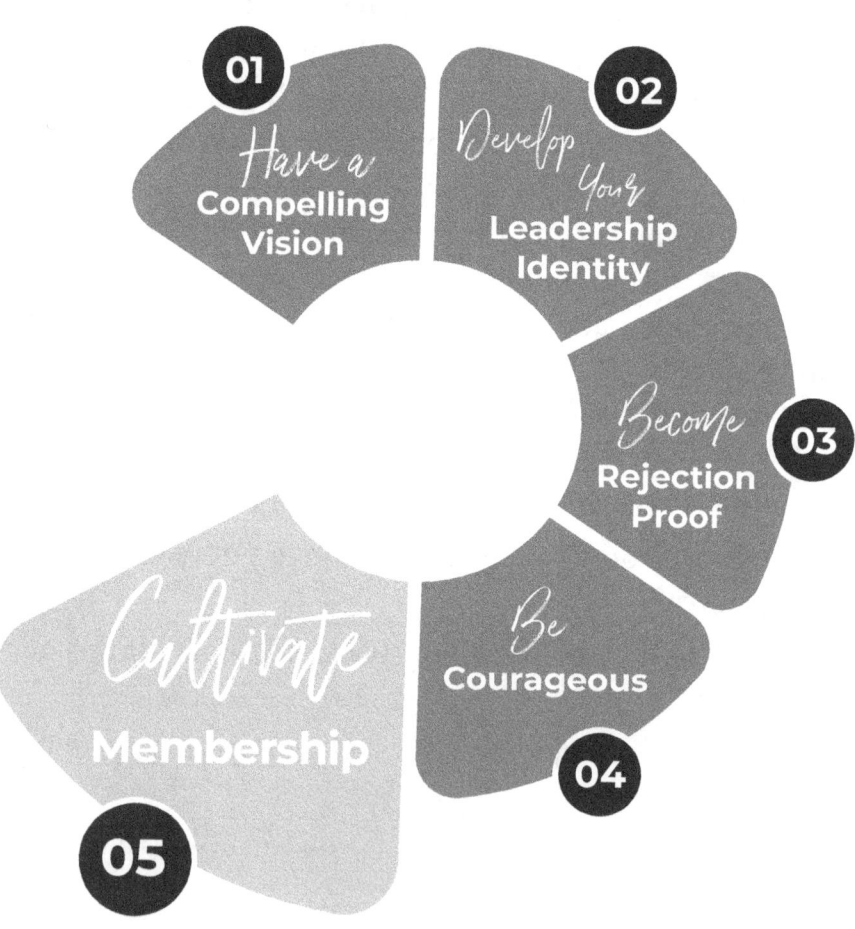

01 Have a Compelling Vision
02 Develop Your Leadership Identity
03 Become Rejection Proof
04 Be Courageous
05 Cultivate Membership

# #5 Cultivate Membership:

The leadership equation is not complete without having people to lead. Your title or position will not engage, energize, and unleash your people's discretionary energy. Gone are the days of command and control and when a leader had to be the smartest person in the room. Remember the wise words of John Maxwell, "No one cares how much you know until they know how much you care." People will not follow you because you tell them. They will follow you because they want to.

Great leaders inspire membership, not followership. For example, there is a difference in mindset in how car owners and renters treat their cars. Followers have no sense of ownership, so they take on a subordinate role. On the other hand, members have an owner's mindset—they are contributors and co-builders of the vision with the leader. So how do leaders cultivate a membership mindset in their teams and organizations?

- **Vision**: It starts with having a compelling vision. According to Mckinsey, since COVID-19, 70% of employees are now demanding purposeful work. Invest time in helping them see how daily jobs make a difference in the world.

## 5 Essential Things Every Leader Must Get Right

- **Trust**: According to the 2021 Edelman Trust Barometer, there is a trust deficit in leadership. To establish your credibility, become a leader people want to follow by closing the say-do gap. If you're going to transition your organization from point A to point B in the shortest possible time, trust is your differentiator. The time to get things done and the cost of doing business are reduced when trust is within a system.

- **Balance**: Focus equal amounts of time on strategy, execution, and culture. The temptation to focus on strategy and execution relative to building a vibrant culture is a big miss. As Peter Drucker puts it, "Culture eats strategy for breakfast."

- **Treat your employees like customers**: Businesses that take their customers for granted become grounded. The more you know your customers, the more you can meet and exceed their needs. Similarly, get to know your employees beyond their ID numbers. Find out what excites and motivates them. Equipping your employees by investing in their growth and development is a win-win strategy.

- **Feedback**: Ask your employees regularly for feedback. It shows that you respect and care about their input. Make sure you thank them for being courageous to give their input. Also, let them know you heard them and share what you will do about their feedback.

The increasing complexity of business challenges, evolving customer needs, and war for talent means that leaders must inspire membership to beat the competition. Also, leaders must be seen as co-partners, not above the team, to successfully attract, build, and activate a membership community.

## Food For Thought

According to an African proverb, 'If you want to walk fast, walk alone, but if you want to walk far, walk together." Different pictures can emerge here, a leader who walks behind, beside, ahead, or above. To cultivate membership, reflect on the following:

- Is my organizational purpose and vision a shared vision?

- Am I planning and informing the team, or am I sharing stories and inspiring the team?

- Do I encourage healthy debates on issues with my team?

- Does my team feel empowered to make decisions in my absence?

- Do I override the decisions my team makes?

- Do I have a lookup culture?

- Do I ask for feedback, admit when I am wrong, or don't have an answer?

## 5 Essential Things Every Leader Must Get Right

01. Have a **Compelling Vision**
02. Develop Your **Leadership Identity**
03. Become **Rejection Proof**
04. Be **Courageous**
05. Cultivate **Membership**

## Closing

Try out this exercise. Imagine it is your last day at the office. You are at your sendoff party. Your boss, direct reports, colleagues, and customers are present. What would you like each of them to say about you? How would you like to be remembered? Write down the themes or values that are emerging from these conversations? Congratulations, you have just created your leadership values. Hold yourself accountable to living them every day. So, on your last day at the office, you can look back at all you have accomplished with your team and say, "I gave it my all. I left nothing on the table, and it was worth it."

# My Action Plan

Congratulations, you have made it this far! As you may know, there is a big gap between knowing and doing. It is applied knowledge that accelerates your growth and development. Take some time to reflect, and answer the following questions:

**What are three insights I am taking away from this book?**
- What are my strengths?
- What are my development opportunities?

**Focus on 1-2 development opportunities at a time:**
- What does success look like?
- What challenges are getting in the way?
- What can I do to turn these challenges into opportunities?
- Who do I need to enlist to accelerate my progress?
- What actions, skills, or experiences do I need to develop or strengthen over the next 90 days?
- What steps can I take in the next 24 hours to start this process?
- How will I measure and track progress?

## CONNECT WITH US

For additional information, scheduling speaking and consulting engagements, please visit **richardosibanjo.com** and email **richard@richardosibanjo.com**.

www.ingramcontent.com/pod-product-compliance
Lightning Source LLC
Chambersburg PA
CBHW070428240526
45472CB00020B/1647